All The Ways I Screwed Up My First Year of Teaching

and How You Can Avoid Doing It, Too

Katrina Ayres

Gary- Thank you for all you do for students!

Katrina :)

ISBN: 1479388955

ISBN-13: 978-1479388950 :

CONTENTS

 INTRODUCTION

Paradise and Reality

How my tropical island dream turns into a big fat hairy nightmare.

Hey, Bruh!'"

"Howzit, Auntie!"

People shouted greetings, waved, and kissed each other as they boarded the little Aloha Airlines prop plane for the thirty-minute flight from Honolulu to Molokai, Hawaii. Thick beautiful pidgin swelled all around me. I understood none of it. Quite a few passengers brought huge fast-food takeout bags on board and crammed duct-taped white foam coolers into the overhead bins.

As we lifted off, I pressed my face to the window. Or I would have, if I could have reached it. A regal-looking Hawaiian auntie wearing a flower lei, colorful muumuu, and large hand-woven hat occupied the seat next to me. I enjoyed the spicy scent of her flowers while I strained to peek around her to get a glimpse of my new island home.

I couldn't wait to start the first chapter of my new adventure as a third grade teacher in Hawaii. I was a brand-new teacher, six months out of college, whose solo teaching experiences consisted of a few hours as a substitute.

Molokai had a chronic teacher shortage. The locals still laugh about one culture-shocked main-lander who climbed off the plane, took one look around, and raced back to the airport to catch the next plane to Honolulu. Although I loved the peaceful feeling of the island the minute I arrived, many young teachers fresh out of college preferred a more urban setting. So the Hawaii Department of Education sent recruiters to teacher colleges on the mainland each year. When they came to my college, I interviewed just for the heck of it, and to my shock, the recruiter hired me on the spot.

Even though I was new to teaching, I had some life experience under my belt before climbing on the plane to Molokai. I had quit my corporate job because I wanted to make a difference in the world instead of shuffling papers from desk to desk for the rest of my life. My husband told me I was a born teacher. Then he said he didn't want me to teach, because it would remind him of his own miserable school experiences. We split up the following year.

To get into the School of Education, I had to complete two years of undergraduate work first, then write essays, participate in numerous interviews, and fill out lengthy applications. No one in our program had a college GPA below 3.0, and most, like me, were straight-A students. The program turned away two people for every person accepted.

Once you were in, you weren't guaranteed to stay

in. About half the students either opted out or failed out. Because of the exclusivity and rigor of my teacher training program, I felt justified thinking I was a better-than-average new teacher. I knew I had a lot to learn, of course, but I had just made it through that horrific program, hadn't I? And I managed to go through a divorce and work to support myself at the same time. If I survived that, I should be able to get through my first year of teaching with no problem at all, right?

Yeah, not so much. I gained thirty pounds and a drinking habit after my first year. After two years I was on antidepressants and close to a nervous breakdown. It was definitely not a good two years of my life, although it did have its moments, such as skinny dipping in the beautiful blue ocean next to a deserted white sand beach.

I learned a lot, though, and I turned it all around in my third and fourth years of teaching, thanks to a **classroom management**[1] *class, support from my*

---

[1] Bold words are in the Glossary of Teacher-Speak on page 105.

church, and the antidepressants I mentioned. The classroom management class was the most important thing. It taught me all the practical skills that had somehow been missing from classes in my teacher education program. Yes, the theoretical stuff is important, but a lot is missing, which leads me to the purpose for this collection of essays.

I don't want anyone to have to go through what I went through in my first two years of teaching. Not only that, but I don't want any students to suffer through a teacher as incompetent as I was. I hope I entertain you (because many of my mistakes are pretty funny, in retrospect) and I hope I give you some practical suggestions and hints.

I am on a mission to help you become the inspirational teacher you know you can be. With that in mind, I dedicate this book to you, and invite you to the sunny red-dirt island of Molokai with me as I showcase all the mistakes I made and explain what I think you can do to avoid them.

I'm going to tell it like it really was for me, which might conflict with what some of the experts say.

I'm not writing a textbook here (because God knows enough textbooks exist in the world already!) I'm just sharing my own experiences with you, hoping they will help.

If your experiences are different, and they probably are, I invite you to contribute your perspective with the Positive Educator Community at Positive TeachingStrategies.com *and at* Facebook.com/PositiveTeachingStrategies. *Please share what you think about my first-year teaching mistakes, as well as any teaching hints to help others in the community. Today's educators need all the help we can get, and we aren't getting it from politicians, parents, or our school districts. It's up to us to help ourselves if we are going to change the world.*

 **CHAPTER 1**

Watch Out, Martha Stewart

Why it's important to stay out of the dangerous, addictive teacher supply store.

andreeamironiuc.com

Before I even buy my one-way ticket to Hawaii, I pack boxes of classroom supplies and mail them to the school where I'll be teaching. When I arrive, a pile of dented, bedraggled boxes awaits me in **the office**. The secretary smiles one of those "if it wasn't my job to be nice to you, I'd probably kill you" smiles and lets me know my classroom is filled with "quite a few" more boxes.

Out of the fifty boxes I sent over, about thirty contain clothes, kitchen supplies, bedding, and other household goods. I stuffed the rest with bulletin board borders, books, posters, maps, photographs, stick-on lettering systems, calendars, and pocket charts. I threw in a few books of worksheets to photocopy, textbooks from teacher college with all their great ideas, and my final **work sample project**—a **unit** on insects. (After all, what's the purpose of doing the work sample project with all its lesson plans and materials lists if I'm not going to teach it in the classroom my first year?) Mostly, though, I packed those boxes full of stuff for setting up my room. The teacher supply store in Oregon loved me!

(For those who don't know, a teacher supply store is an irresistible combination of office supply store, book store, and gift shop for teachers. It stocks every conceivable cutesy prize, poster, game, book, or manual a teacher could ever want. Don't go there! It's dangerous and highly addictive.)

I open the bulging boxes and get ready for the

first day of school. I scrub counters and create clever bulletin boards. I plaster every available wall space with a colorful poster or banner declaring, *This is a Learning Zone, There is No 'I' in TEAM,* and *You Only Lose When You Quit.* Of course I hang the obligatory **alphabet chart** over the chalkboard.

(For those of you too young to remember, a "chalkboard" was a green piece of slate or slate-like material teachers wrote on with chalk a million years ago before whiteboards, SMART boards, and document cameras. At the end of the day, a thick layer of chalk dust covered all teachers' hands and clothing unless they were lucky enough to own a little metal holder for their chalk.)

I now realize none of the decorating was necessary. None of it! Sure, cute little pillows for the reading area are nice, and it's fun to have some color in the room, but beyond someplace for the students to sit and a place for their supplies, none of it is important for learning.

The most important thing to do in the weeks before school is plan. And whatever you do, don't "plan" the way I did. I filled the first two weeks of squares in my new teacher plan book (another $12.95 dropped at the teacher supply store) with getting-to-know-you activities and games. I figured the rest would fall into place after that. (After all, I had my insect unit, remember?)

I will give my New Teacher Self a little credit. I thought everything fell into place after the first two weeks because my **cooperating teacher** made it look like that's what happened. She had opened school for about twenty years and knew the rhythm and sequence of her year. She did all the planning before I even met her, and when I showed up, eager and enthusiastic, she gave me a bulletin board project to burn off some of my excess energy. She told me how she planned the year, but I sort of forgot in my initial enthusiasm and teacher-supply-store-induced adrenaline rush.

If I could travel back in time and have a little talk with my New Teacher Self, I would give her a big hug and some hard-earned advice:

Forget about decorating. Get the student text-book (Gasp! The textbook! How old fashioned!) for the subjects you teach. Flip to the table of contents and look at the topics and the order they come in. Make a list.

Make an appointment with an experienced teacher at your grade level or subject. The best option is someone at your school, preferably next door to you. If you are the only one in your school, reach out to an experienced teacher at a nearby school. Show her the list or textbook and ask her which of the topics she teaches and which she leaves out. Ask her which month she usually teaches each topic. Write this down! She may even have a schedule. If she does, by all means steal it!

Get that new teacher plan book out. Fill in all the dates. Mark out the holidays and vacations. Make a list of the topics for each month on a sticky note and attach it to the appropriate page of your plan book.

Outline the first month's lessons. You don't need

to create every handout and activity, but know the main projects. Include room procedure lessons and team building activities, but intersperse them with **subject area content**.

Plan the heck out of the first two weeks, including handouts, activities, and worksheets. (Swipe these from the experienced teacher if you can.) Don't worry about preparing too much work. Readying more activities than you need is much better than finishing a two-day lesson in thirty minutes and trying to make something up on the spot.

If your principal or other teachers pressure you to decorate, hang *Student Work* and *We Love to Learn* signs on your bulletin boards. On the first day of school, you will identify The Student Who Finishes Everything Early. Ask her to staple your class's first assignment to the bulletin boards. Done. Go take a nap.

Above all I would tell my New Teacher Self to take it easy on herself. You don't have to be perfect or know everything, nor does your room have to be a work of art. Spend your best effort learning the most effective ways to teach your content, and later you can create a beautiful learning kingdom with all the bells and whistles.

 **CHAPTER 2**

I Can Do It All

In which I microwave paper, battle the Monster
Copier, and never, never stop working, ever.

I stand on the counter about a week before the first day of school in my bare feet and my shorts, wielding a stapler, singing along to Bonnie Raitt, and stapling in time. I've been in Hawaii three weeks and I'm tired and punchy. I work in my room eight or nine hours nearly every day in addition to unpacking and settling in at home. And of course I spend a little bit of time going to the beach and exploring the island. But it's crunch time now. School starts next Monday.

I spend time each day in the copy room, which is approximately the size of a large walk-in closet, learning the idiosyncrasies of the evil office machinery. One of the photocopiers (which I will nickname the Monster Copier to avoid a lawsuit from the manufacturer) imprints the original document onto a strange transparent piece of paper called a "master" which looks and feels like a cross between waxed paper and tissue paper. The Monster Copier makes copies from the masters (if it's in the mood,) crumples the used masters, and crams them into a little box. Every couple of hours I have to empty the little box, a procedure which almost always results in black ink streaks on my hands, legs, and clothing.

The Monster Copier also jams a lot, and when it does, I have to open a mysterious series of doors and trays in order and pull and/or crank various levers in different directions until I find and release the ink-soaked paper and pry it off the roller (smearing me once again with smelly black ink.) After I follow all the weird directions, close all the drawers and doors, and push the reset button, the red light still flashes and the Monster Copier still refuses to work. It's like a really cruel real-life video game or an experiment designed to test the intelligence of lab rats before rewarding them with a piece of cheese.

The regular photocopier jams also, and it sometimes prints on only the top half of the paper. Other times it comes out gray, with the words showing faintly like a shadow. I later learn this happens because the paper absorbs humidity from the air. The other teachers suggest I microwave the paper to get the moisture out before sending it through the copier. Who knew the microwave was an essential piece of office equipment?

After battling the copy machines, moving desks and bookcases, and hanging up posters all day, I spend my evenings working at home. I trim laminated materials, color posters, plan lessons, and create worksheets to photocopy the next day (if the copier gods are smiling.)

If this sounds like it takes a long time, you're

right. It does. It takes me one to two hours of preparation work (or more) for every hour spent actually delivering the lesson to the students. In the typical six-hour school day, I get one hour without students (usually spent in some sort of meeting,) which leaves five hours to teach. If your math teachers did their jobs, you can easily figure out that I have two to ten hours of prep work to do each day after my students go home. Once I take time to sleep, I have almost zero time for anything else, such as grocery shopping.

Still, I'm going to do whatever it takes to be a great teacher, and I'm not going to cut corners. I put in the hours, lugging a large canvas tote filled with work everywhere I go. Other teachers tell me it goes with the territory. You have to spend a lot of time in your first year and any time you switch grade levels or subjects. This is true. However, it is not necessary to spend every waking hour working.

The secret? Borrow, work cooperatively, outsource, and make the kids do more work than you.

Borrow lessons and worksheets instead of creating them yourself. If you are teaching a skill or topic, I guarantee you someone else in your building or online has taught it before you. Reach out to other teachers who teach or have taught your same subject and grade level and ask what they use. You can even use the teacher supply store or websites with downloadable materials as long as you don't distract yourself with cool lessons with lots of bells and whistles that aren't in your **curriculum**. Make it a habit to share anything you find with other teachers. This is good karma and will encourage them to do the same for you. (Not in a smartass, I-know-everything-even-though-I'm-a-first-year-teacher way. In a helpful, humble way.)

Work cooperatively as a team with others in your grade level to make copies for each other. It's always faster to make fifty copies of one worksheet than to make twenty-five copies of two worksheets. Better yet, find one reliable parent to make copies and prepare materials for your whole team. Designate a space where you will all put work that needs to be done so the parent can stop in, grab everyone's work, and get busy without supervision.

Don't hesitate to outsource. People like to help. Parents, grandparents, aunties and uncles (yours and your students') like to trim lamination, hang bulletin boards, and color. Students will fight over who gets to use the stapler, label books, and sharpen pencils. After your first year, ask your former students to come back and help before school or during recess. Show your appreciation with stickers or other treats for the kids and Starbucks cards for the adults.

Give the copy machine a rest every once in awhile. Ask the students to copy down math problems, reading group discussion questions, writing prompts, and **graphic organizers** from the board or projector. You will save time, save paper, and teach your students an essential school skill. Shift the responsibility for student materials to the students as much as possible. Ask The Student Who Finishes Everything Early to sort or organize. This is a good life skill, and she will love to do it.

If your employers wanted a paper hanger, copy machine guru, or laminating pro they would have hired one. You have a college degree and specialized training in teaching. Use your time, as much as possible, to teach.

 **CHAPTER 3**

The Heroic Hoarder

In which I reminisce about mimeographs, breathe mildew, and wish I had listened to Miss Iaea.

andreeamironiuc.com

The door to my neighboring classroom is open! I've been waiting two weeks for this moment, wondering what the other third grade teacher will be like. I peek in the door. A vaguely mildewy scent permeates the air. Desks, tables, and piles of books crowd every available horizontal surface. Gravity-defying posters, calendars, and memos hang five to seven layers deep on the walls. I don't see the teacher anywhere, so I turn to go.

"Aloha!" I turn back and see movement in the far corner of the room. A short solid woman with straight black hair, a round Hawaiian face, and dark crinkly eyes greets me. I pick my way across the room to meet her, bumping into several desks and tables as I go.

Miss Iaea (her name strangely lacking in consonants) introduces herself and gives me an inventory list. Apparently I am expected to count and log every single book, globe, map, and piece of furniture in my room. My stomach drops. She "helps" me more by showing me her yellowing, brittle teacher books and offering to let me borrow her beginning-of-the-year worksheet masters which were "run off" on a mimeograph machine back in the 1960s.

(For those of you too young to know, "mimeographing" was the way teachers made copies a million years ago before the invention of the copy machine. The bluish-purple ink had a distinctive smell that faded over time. As a student, I loved it when my teacher waited until the last minute to mimeograph because the worksheet would be warm, fresh, and strong. I would press the paper up to my face, inhale deeply, and get a little high. Oh yeah!)

I escape Miss Iaea's room as soon as I politely can, back to my perfect bulletin boards and Teacher Supply Store Heaven. On the phone that evening, my college friends and I laugh at her outdated methods and scorn her authoritarian style.

I sure wish I could go back and change all that, because I could have saved myself a ton of time and effort if I had listened to her.

Miss Iaea may have been old-fashioned, but she had thirty years of teaching experience. As I now know, if you can last thirty years in the classroom, you probably have at least a few survival skills under your belt (or in the case of Miss Iaea, under your muumuu.) She knew (and told me) that students don't really need to go to the bathroom whenever they want. She had a gigantic store of age-appropriate educational activities I could have adapted from their dusty mimeographed format instead of making everything up. She knew the rhythm of the school year and where her **curriculum** fit in with the rest of the school.

Most importantly, she knew the community. She knew where the kids lived; in fact, she had taught some of their parents. She knew which families would be supportive and which would not, and she knew the best way to approach each family. Miss Iaea was a treasure trove of information, and I sure wish I had listened to her.

If I could give my New Teacher Self some advice, here's what I would tell her.

New Teacher Self, take the brittle books and mimeographed materials Miss Iaea is so generously offering you. Make enough copies of them for both of your classes (thus ridding the world of the mimeographs and expanding your own resources.) Implement her activities in your own fun updated style, take notes on how to improve each lesson, and make the necessary changes the following year. If you decide not to use some of her materials or teach some of her **units**, don't tell her. If you find something works really well, be sure to let her know.

Master teachers are a valuable resource, and they are also human. Be humble, be nice, and above all listen! You'll be glad you did.

 **CHAPTER 4**

Student Teacher Superstar Becomes New Teacher Train Wreck

In which I learn I'm not as amazing as I thought I was.

I gaze out over the sea of little faces shining up at me as I read aloud from a book about insects. All is peaceful and calm. Moments earlier **the office** called to cancel an assembly, and I needed to quickly adjust. No problem for me, amazing **student teacher** that I am. I can handle anything. I'm actually probably more like a "real" teacher than a student teacher. True, my **cooperating teacher** is in the room, but she's not doing anything except smiling at me from time to time.

A parent of one of the more wiggly students walks into the room. The **master teacher** greets her and invites her into the hallway for a little chat. Later when the students are working on another project, she introduces us. I invite the parent to participate in class and show her the box of volunteer work. Soon she is busy cutting out materials. I'm such a great teacher! Even the parents love me!

One of the students in "my" class is a runner. At six years old, he's a refugee from a horrible situation in the Middle East, and he freaks out and runs out of the room any time he gets a chance. My master teacher attends meetings after school about him all the time. Other teachers in the **staff room** tell me they can't figure out how I can handle it. I lower my eyes modestly. "It's not really that bad," I say.

One day I forget to plan a lesson because I took a college exam the previous day. I don't worry about it too much. I go to the cupboard of ready-to-go **filler**

activities and pick one. No problem! Most people would be overwhelmed, going to college full-time, working part time, and student teaching. Not me! I have it handled!

Fast forward to halfway through my first year of teaching in Hawaii. The parents are upset with me, no one volunteers in my room, the students are far from **angelic**, and my desk is a huge volcano of paper spewing student work and lesson plans everywhere.

What happened?

At first, I blame the school community. The principal isn't supportive, the schedule is impossible, I don't have enough **plan time**, I don't have enough materials, and on and on. Later I blame the parents. The parents don't provide enough discipline for their kids at home, so they don't know how to act at school. Parents are prejudiced against me because I'm a "foreigner" from the mainland. Parents are too lazy to help out in the classroom.

None of this is true. The truth is I wasn't nearly as experienced a teacher as I thought I was, and I made a lot of mistakes an experienced teacher would know how to avoid. The support provided for me during student teaching was invisible to me until years later.

Before I took over her class, my master teacher set up **discipline expectations** for the students and taught them how she expected them to behave. She arranged the classroom to support the students in their learning and established the curriculum long before she gave me the insect **unit** to teach. True, I watched her, and she graciously explained what she was doing, but watching a demonstration is not the same as making it happen. Think of a professional basketball player dribbling between his legs, floating effortlessly to the hoop past three defenders, and making a slam-dunk. He can tell you all about his training program. He can even break down the moves for you and explain it all step by step. That doesn't mean you can duplicate his results when he hands you the basketball.

If the master teacher is any good, she isn't going to let you fail, either. When you make a mistake, she'll help you fix it, both for your sake and for the sake of her students. It's like a parent teaching a little kid to swim. The kid might think he's swimming on his own, but no one's going to let him drown. In the same way, my master teacher headed off many problems for me before they even developed. While she was in the back of the room smiling at me, she was working to create those filler activities for the closet. She was developing intervention strategies for the refugee kid, setting up the volunteer area, tactfully explaining my presence to the wiggly student's parent, and finding insect books for the class library.

I'm glad I had a positive student teaching experience. I wouldn't change anything about it, because it created in me the vision of myself as a successful teacher, a vision I clung to during the tough times. But I do wish I could somehow have waved a magic wand in front of my New Teacher Self before she started teaching on her own and reveal to her how much support her master teacher provided. I think it would have changed her attitude and helped her avoid many of the other mistakes she made her first year.

 **CHAPTER 5**

Blowing Bubbles

Students are not like goldfish, and why this is important to you.

andreeamironiuc.com

It's my last semester of college and I'm studying one of my textbooks. "Whenever possible, students should be given many learning choices to honor their diversity and encourage them to create their own meaning," it says.

Out comes the yellow pen. "Yes, yes," I murmur, highlighting away.

I drift away in a daydream. A busy hum fills my

future classroom. Students are focused and enthusiastically **engaged** at learning centers. Eyes shining, a girl shows me a story she just created in the writing center. I praise her work, and she runs off to create a cover with stamps and markers. Two boys practice math facts by multiplying the dots on dominoes and recording their answers. At the art center, students create beautiful mixed-media projects. The students flow from center to center as they complete their work. They are empowered! Engaged! Enthusiastic! Never in my classroom are students bored and discouraged about school. I nurture their natural desire to learn (another phrase I highlight in the book.)

Halfway through my first year of teaching, I wonder what happened. The art table is crowded as usual, and everyone fights over the glitter glue stick. No one ever visits the spelling center. Two boys hit each other with dominoes. The math flash cards are dented and half the deck is lost.

At the end of the day I go over the "work" the students produced. Five projects were turned in and four of them are two-dimensional daisy-like flower drawings. One is a "book" with fifty pages. Two sheets have writing on them and the rest seem to be filled with scribbling. I gave the students plenty of learning opportunities, but have they learned anything? It doesn't look like it. What happened to their natural desire to learn and create?

New Teacher Self, if children naturally learned everything they need to learn on their own, school (and parents) would be unnecessary. Unlike goldfish, which emerge from their eggs already knowing how to do everything, human children need direction and guidance. It's hard to create a wonderful writing project if you don't know how to write a sentence. It's difficult to create a mixed-media work of art if you only know how to draw two-dimensional daisy-like flowers.

Students need **direct instruction** as well as the freedom to experiment with their newfound skills.

Please don't let them flit from activity to activity without direction and expect them to learn. Instead, teach them a specific skill and help them practice. If you are using learning centers, let them know the purpose of each activity and when it needs to be completed.

Sure, give them choices. Let them decide if they want to do the odd-numbered math problems, or the even-numbered ones. Let them choose which **graphic organizer** to use when creating a storyboard for their writing. Let them decide if they'd like to record their answers in purple pencil or blue pencil. Let them decide if they'd like to do the spelling activity before or after they write in their journals. Let them choose the theme for their poem.

Your job is to facilitate learning. Learning means growing, changing, and sharpening skills over the years. Provide the activities needed for growth and watch your students' creativity bloom. It will be much more beautiful than a two-dimensional daisy-like flower.

 **CHAPTER 6**

The Dreaded W-Word

Who tells you not to say it, and why I think it's okay.

After fifteen minutes of strenuous effort, Jennie hands me her math paper. I quickly scan it. Not a single correct answer. I point to one of the problems. "Seven plus two is five. That's an interesting answer. How did you get it?"

"I won add 'em!"

"Show me what you did."

"I did seven plus two and get five. Is it right,

Teacher?" Jennie's huge dark brown eyes rake my face for clues.

"What do you think?"

"Dunno."

"If you had two **Pokémon** cards and I gave you seven more, how many would you have?"

"Don't like Pokémon."

"Just pretend. How many would you have?"

"Eight?" The eyes study me closely. "Ten? Nine?" I must have shown a hint of a smile. "Nine! It's nine!" she shrieks, and runs off to change the answer. I'm proud I've once again guided little Jennie into finding the answer for herself without ever once saying the dreaded W-word. You know... wrong.

My well-meaning college instructors and textbook authors went on at length about the damaging effects of criticism. When students feel incapable, they lose **motivation** and stop trying. Their math answers need not always be correct as long as students can explain their thinking. Inventive spelling (otherwise known as spelling words wrong) is fine —

they will naturally acquire standard spelling (ie, spelling words right) later on.

Another danger lies in telling students they're smart. It is better to praise their effort so they will equate hard work with success. Students should learn to evaluate and check their own work instead of relying on adults to tell them if their work is good. Motivation should come from within the child instead of from adult manipulation.

With these words ringing in my ears, I vow not to be a hypercritical, restrictive teacher, damaging my students with criticism and rewards. Students in my class will be empowered! Motivated! Creative! Expressive! The trouble is I translate this into never ever, no matter what, correcting the students' work.

Here's the truth. Nothing will stop young children from trying to please adults. It is a hardwired survival instinct. Refusing to let them know when they have done something wrong just causes them to keep trying different things until you look happy. And letting them think their work is right when it isn't is just irresponsible. Correcting students' work can and should be done with tact and compassion, of course, but accepting incorrect work only allows students to practice doing it wrong (notice I used the W-word) over and over again.

If I had a chance to have a little talk with my New Teacher Self, here's what I'd say:

New Teacher Self, your teaching method is WRONG! Wrong, wrong, wrong, wrong, wrong! No, I'm just kidding. What I would really say is:

You can correct students gently by saying, "That's not quite right," or "I'm not sure that makes sense," or "Everything looks good, except for..." You don't have to bark out corrections right and left. Find a balance! Students may initially feel bad about getting something wrong but they will feel worse about not knowing the skills. The best self-esteem builder of all is confidence. Help the students learn from their mistakes instead of pretending they don't make them.

Encourage students to look for mistakes in your work. Make a game out of it by making mistakes on purpose and rewarding students who find them. They will learn it's okay to be wrong as long as you admit it and learn from it. Refusing to talk about errors makes mistakes seem shameful and embarrassing rather than the opportunity for learning that they are.

It's okay to give a student a pat on the back for doing something correctly. No matter what the "experts" say, all people (even kids) like recognition for doing something right. A sincere compliment won't hurt your students, and neither will a gentle correction.

 **CHAPTER 7**

Sand in My Plan Book

Why I advise against laminating at the beach.

I'm lying on my stomach on a deck chair by a beautiful almost-deserted pool at a golf resort in Hawaii. I sip a rum and coke from my plastic water bottle. The sun massages my back, and the breeze rustles the palm fronds above me. Occasionally I hear the distant crash of a wave on the beach. I breathe in the spicy scent of red dirt, salt, a little chlorine, perfume from the plumeria... and sigh and flip the page in my lesson plan book to the next week.

I would dearly love to drift off to sleep and unwind after my stressful week of teaching, but I can't. I'm panicking about all the work I still have to do. It's Saturday, and I know if I don't get my weekly plans done today, I won't have time to prepare my materials tomorrow for class on Monday. But I refuse to live in Hawaii and spend my entire weekend inside. So the crossbar of the deck chair digs into my hip bones as I write in the plan book and try not to spill my drink on it.

I bet you've never seen anyone trimming laminated materials at a beach resort, but if you visited the beach where I hung out on the weekends, that's exactly what you would have seen. I could do it all — grade papers, write progress reports, plan, and prepare materials. At first this might seem kind of cool. If you have to work anyway, why not do it at the pool or at the beach?

Here's why not. First of all, remember that rum and coke I mentioned? How accurate was my grading? Was I designing my best lessons? What about the sleepiness factor of lying in the sun or the many distractions I had to overcome at the beach?

And what about lugging my bulging canvas bag of work around with me everywhere? It was a huge burden, physically and mentally. I never left it behind, even on weekends and vacations. I was exhausted, cranky, and depressed, chained to a never-ending treadmill of work.

The advice I would give my New Teacher Self now would save her a lot of stress, time, and medical bills, and make her a much better teacher. Sadly, she probably wouldn't listen, but I sure wish she would. Just in case, here it is.

New Teacher Self, I know you have a lot to do. I know you have more to do than any mortal human can possibly get done during the workweek. But you still need time off. In the long run it will make you faster and better at what you do, because you won't be working in a bleary, sleep-deprived, stress-induced fog. You will be able to respond better to the students, which will reduce the amount of time you spend putting out fires in the classroom, calling parents, conferencing with the school counselor about students, and filling out discipline reports. Once you have better control of the classroom, you will be able to plan and do paperwork while the students work independently. So here's the rule. Work at work and be home when you're home. Pretend your principal forbids you to take any work home and figure out how to get it all done at school.

I know this is shocking advice, and I didn't attempt it until a friend suggested it in my sixth year of teaching. I didn't even think it was possible. Nevertheless, I made a deal with myself to try it for two weeks and see what happened. At first I didn't know what to do with myself at home if I wasn't working. It was especially hard to keep from working when I thought about all I had to do, but I persevered.

At first I worked much longer hours at school,

leaving at 7:00 or 8:00 at night and going in to school on the weekends. Later I found I could work less because I stopped wasting time on unnecessary activities, stopped reinventing everything, and started delegating. In short, I found better, more efficient ways to work because I was more rested and less distracted.

Give it a try. Your students deserve a more relaxed you, and your family deserves to see you once in awhile. Who knows? You may even get a chance to figure out what everyone else means when they talk about having "hobbies."

 **CHAPTER 8**

Tarzan, Monkeys, and Colorful Birds

Who cares if it's not in the curriculum?

andreeamironiuc.com

I'm wandering the aisles of the teacher supply store in a poster-induced daze, fingering wall charts, games, and markers of all types; dipping my nose into all the wonderful lesson plan books; and dreaming of the day I will have a class of my own. Lesson plan books are especially attractive with their ready-made worksheets and full-blown **integrated units** on all kinds of interesting topics such as The

Human Body (at least thirty different books) and The Universe (fifty books, plus puzzles, glow-in-the-dark stars, posters, games, models, computer games, and craft activities.)

I fall in love with The Rainforest, although I'm not sure why. Maybe I have a subconscious desire to be Tarzan and yodel while I swing through the forest on a vine. Or maybe it's all the cute monkeys and colorful birds. Whatever the reason, I decide to teach a rainforest **unit** to my future students.

To support my rainforest unit, I buy three different rainforest lesson plan books and about a zillion rainforest books for kids—rainforest stories, rainforest poetry books, rainforest popup books, rainforest song books, and rainforest giant books. Oh, and videos too. (For those too young to know, when I say "video" I don't mean an MP4 or WMP file you watch on your phone. Once upon a time videos used to be black plastic rectangular cases you slid into a "VCR" and watched on the television you checked out from the school library and rolled into your classroom on a cart.)

So what if there's no rainforest in the third grade **curriculum**? So what if the other third grade teacher doesn't teach **thematic units**? My students are going to be so jazzed up about The Rainforest they will naturally learn all the skills in the curriculum quickly and painlessly.

Since I spent so much money purchasing materials and shipping them to Hawaii, and since I spent so much time previewing the videos, reading the books, practicing the songs, and reviewing all the lessons in the unit guidebook, I am not going to teach this unit for only a week. It lasts more than a month. By the end of it my room actually becomes a rainforest, complete with a **butcher paper** river and butcher paper trees. The students create three-dimensional animals by cutting out two identical animal drawings, coloring them, stapling them together, and stuffing them with more paper. (The irony of using so much paper in a unit essentially about the importance of trees to our planet only occurred to me years later.)

Why did I invest all this time and money on

something I wasn't paid by the good taxpayers of Hawaii to teach? Because I love to be creative. I love fresh ideas and new ways of doing things. I want to inspire my students to love learning as much as I do. And none of that is wrong. In fact, it's great. It just needs a little redirecting.

Here's what I would tell my New Teacher Self.

New Teacher Self, use the teacher supply store (and lesson plan databases) for ideas, but don't buy anything (tempting as it may be) until you know what the other teachers are doing and what materials the school already has. You don't get extra credit for spending more money or effort on your lessons. Students may feel as excited and **motivated** by simple things (like a special marker) as they do by participating in a fancy rainforest unit. Your principal won't give you extra credit either, especially if you don't teach what you are supposed to teach. Take the money you save and pay your school loans, pay the rent, or pamper yourself a little.

Start small and give yourself a chance to see what is effective and what isn't. It's hard to abandon a gigantic complicated unit you have spent a lot of time and money preparing for, but it's not such a big deal to find a new approach for a single lesson that flopped. Once you discover which lessons work for you and your students, you can combine and/or extend those fantastic lessons into a unit.

Pour your amazing creativity and energy into fun, inspiring lessons about the math, spelling, reading, social studies, or science objectives you are supposed to teach. If you can create a great lesson about what the students are actually supposed to learn, everyone wins! Realize that the material you teach your students may not be fresh and new to you, but it's new to them. Try to remember the ah-ha moment when you learned it for the first time and recreate that sense of wonder and enthusiasm when you teach it to your students. Buying a bunch of fancy stuff is expensive. Watching students become inspired is free—and also priceless.

 **CHAPTER 9**

Teddy Bear Picnic

In which I decorate lettering, draw curlicues, and deliver an adorable math-free math lesson.

My teddy bear doesn't like pants.

Note: If you are a high school teacher you can skip this chapter, unless you just want to laugh at me.

I gather materials for a math lesson on combinations. Graph paper, check. Pencils, check. Work sheet for recording data, check. Teddy bears and teddy bear clothing, check.

What a cute idea! Use teddy bear outfits to illustrate the idea of combinations! How many outfits can the bear make with three shirts and two pairs of pants? What if we add a couple of hats?

I make copies of all the bears and sets of clothing for each student, plus my larger Demonstration Bear and Clothing Set, which I color and decorate with little logos and flowers before laminating it. I make the worksheets, humming to myself as I decorate the lettering with little dots to make it fancy, and add a curlicue border. It takes several hours to get ready, but it sure is cute!

Now it's time for the actual lesson. I instruct the students to color and cut out all the bears and their clothing and finish the math worksheet. The markers and scissors come out. Soon the room hums with busy energy.

At the end of math about half of the students are through coloring. The shirts all have complicated flower patterns like Aloha shirts, the hats contain detailed representations of sports logos, and the pants sport artful patches and strategically placed holes. No math done, but it sure is cute!

The next day we have a discussion about combinations using the Large Demonstration Bear. "Who wants to make an outfit for the bear?" Hands wave, and Jennie is chosen.

"OK Jennie, create an outfit for the bear using a shirt, pants, and a hat."

"Don't want no hat."

"The bear needs a shirt, pants, and a hat for every outfit."

"The bear doesn't like hats."

Kaden pipes up. "My bear doesn't like shirts."

Two boys in the back giggle that their bears don't like pants. My teeth clinch, but I refrain from yelling, show the class how to fill out the **graphic organizer**, and send the students to their desks to work. The crayons immediately come out and the decorating resumes.

"The time for coloring is over. Today we're making outfits."

"My bear isn't cut out yet."

"Fine! Cut out your bear, but no coloring."

"My bear is almost colored. See, Teacher? I just have one spot left."

My cute activity is out of control. I call the class back to the carpet and the students fill in their charts, following me. To finish up, I staple the Large Demonstration Bear to the wall, surrounded by student-decorated graphic organizers. Do the students learn anything about combinations? Not so much. But it's so cute!

All right New Teacher Self, I'm glad you want don't want stark, ugly, boring materials, and I'm glad you want to **engage** students and capture their attention. I'm even glad you want to nurture the creative, artistic side of your class and relate what they learn to their lives. After all this isn't a prison, and these are children. However, "cute" can be like morning glories or ivy taking over a whole lawn. Use a little restraint. You'll be glad you did.

 **CHAPTER 10**

Around the World With Thirty Students

Entertainers, actors, and movie producers do it.
Why you shouldn't.

andreeamironiuc.com

If that teacher would just make math more interesting, the students in her class wouldn't act up all the time."

How many times have you heard this? I hear it from parents, from students, from principals, and even from other teachers. All humans have experienced an instructor so boring our brains melted away and leaked out our ears. Who can blame students for acting up in a situation like that? A spit wad hitting the teacher's ear at least adds a little drama.

As a new teacher I decide boredom is not going to happen in my class. My eager students will look up in surprise when it's time for recess. "What, already?" they will say. "Couldn't we stay in to finish our work?"

To make sure my class is never boring I design lots of lessons using M&Ms, dice, dominoes, and popup books. I read with a dra-MAT-ic voice and utilize games. Around the World is a favorite. Maybe you've played it. The teacher holds up a math flash card and two students compete to see who can be the first to call out the answer. The winner gets to move on to the next student, and the ultimate winner is the one who can make it all the way around the room. My students love Around the World, and so do I (not much lesson **planning**). It's entertaining and suspenseful. Why, then, do they still act up?

It's because entertainment is not the same as engagement.

Students are **engaged** when they are actively involved in an activity. They are entertained when something has their attention. Engagement is active, but entertainment is passive. It's not a bad idea to entertain, but engagement is so much better.

How many students are engaged in the Around the World game? The one that's challenging and the one being challenged—two out of thirty kids. Maybe one or two others are engaged, such as the one who knows all the math facts, and is feeding them to his friends in exchange for the dessert from their lunches. The audience may be entertained by the suspense of the competition, but it's like watching TV. No participation is required.

Fancy materials are fine, but they don't guarantee engagement either. In fact, sometimes they pretty much guarantee distraction. Students can use dominoes in ways that don't involve performing math operations with the dots, believe me.

Students misbehave for many reasons. Only one of them is boredom. Others can be lack of sleep, hunger, the need for attention, curiosity about what will happen if a "rule" is broken, revenge, **impulsiveness**, ignorance of expectations, and many others. Yes, make your lessons interesting, but don't expect it to guarantee **angelic behavior**.

Don't expect students to behave better during fancy or unusual lessons. In fact, students are likely to act up to find **behavior limits** for the new activity. Many of your students like their routines and hate change (just like many adults.) It's fine to use innovative activities, but just make sure you lay a good foundation and teach expectations carefully. Also, don't feel guilty for planning a "plain" lesson every once in awhile. If you have a mixture of "plain" and "exciting" lessons, the exciting ones will be even more stimulating.

Student involvement creates student engagement. The people who are working are the people who are learning. If you work hard to read in a dramatic voice, you learn more than your audience. In Around the World, the teacher and the two competing students are learning (unless one student isn't even trying because he knows he doesn't have a chance against your star math student. In that case two people are learning, you and the star math student. And since both of you already know your math facts, what's the point?)

Realize you won't be more entertaining than 3D TV, video games, the latest iPad app, the soccer World Cup, or American Idol. Your job is not to out-entertain but to help the students learn and feel great about themselves for learning. Strive to get as many students as possible involved in the lesson, not provide the most over-the-top drama.

Not every student will love every lesson, but every lesson has the potential to awaken a lifelong passion in at least one student. Let your passion and enthusiasm for learning shine through whenever you can and you will not need the gimmicks.

 **CHAPTER 11**

The True Meaning of Diversity

In which I force my students to paste their body
parts into a giant book.

andreeamironiuc.com

One day at the teacher supply store, I stumble across *The Book of Me*. It's about diversity and the way people come in all colors, shapes, and sizes. Noses are different shapes. Ears stick out or not, lobes are attached or detached. Humans are varying shades of brown. I'm experiencing all the beautiful diverse cultures of Hawaii, and along comes an amazing book to sum it all up! How fantastic!

"Kids need to learn they are great just the way they are," I think. "We're going to read that book for Read-Aloud Time." I read the book. It's such a beautiful moment, I don't want it to end. I ask the students to journal about this life-changing, awe-inspiring idea. Their responses aren't that inspiring. Maybe they don't get the point. How can I drive home this super-important concept? Ooooh! We can make a **class book**!

Teacher supply store memories flood over me and I lose all control. I design a gigantic book from tag board and O-rings. One day the students draw their eyes and paste them on the page of eyes. The next day they recreate their ears, the next day their hair, and so on. I hound them for days to get all their body parts glued on the appropriate pages. I don't want anyone's ankle left out, for godsake! When the pages are finished, I laminate each one and clamp them together with the O-rings.

I heft *Our Class Book of Us* onto a chair for the Great Unveiling, savoring every word and every picture. I look up from the pages with a smile that quickly fades. Kaden draws a car, Jennie braids Michelle's hair, Pililua reads a comic book, and Matthew designs a paper airplane. Another two-week lesson plan flop. I quietly add the book to our classroom library, where it gathers dust because it's too heavy for the students to lift out of the book bin.

It's fine to be enthusiastic and passionate about what you like, but don't assume the same fire burns in your students. And for heaven's sake, don't create a two-week unit about something you love but the students don't care about, especially if it's not even in the **curriculum**. If a concept or idea doesn't connect with your students, don't force the issue. Instead, be on the lookout for ideas that fascinate your students. If you become aware of a student's passion that's not in your curriculum, tactfully offer the opportunity to write about it or suggest a book on the subject. You'll be surprised what students will do when they have a passion.

Marcus, a drug baby with the wildest hair I've ever seen, severe ADD, and the literacy level of a kindergartener, taught himself to read in two weeks. He wanted to read a children's chess strategy book so he could beat his older brother. I started reading chess books along with him and now get cranky if I don't play chess every day.

Listen to your students and help them gain the reading, writing, and research skills they will need to follow their own passions. They will be more successful in school and in life. And who knows? You may develop a new interest of your own, as I did with chess.

 **CHAPTER 12**

The Golden-Feathered Pen

I learn that making third graders sign a poster
doesn't guarantee they will behave.

andreeamironiuc.com

I lift a beautiful golden-feathered pen from the millionth box I unpack, take it out of its elegant case, and sign my name a couple of times. Ahh bliss! The pen reminds me to create my Class Rules poster. Out come the gold stick-on letters and white poster board. An hour later I proudly hang the "Be Kind, Be Safe, Be Respectful" poster in the front of the room.

On the first day of school, I gather my students next to the poster and we have a little talk. I give examples of safety, kindness, and **respect**. After the discussion each student solemnly signs the poster with the special pen. I naïvely think this little ceremony will imprint the importance of the rules in the minds of the students.

The next day Kaden pulls Jennie's hair. "Kaden, is that Kind?" I ask, pointing to the poster. Kaden looks confused. His head swivels to see what I'm pointing to. He looks back at me and shrugs.

"Kaden, come with me. Look here on the poster. Where is your name?"

"Right there, Teacher."

"Did you mean it when you signed the rules?" He nods.

"What do you think you should do now?"

He looks at me for a beat or two. "Math?"

I take a deep breath. "Kaden, what do you think you should do about Jennie?"

Eyes dart to Jennie. Shrug.

"Kaden, you pulled Jennie's hair. Was that

Kind?"

"No." Kaden is an **impulsive** eight-year-old. Kindness is probably not on his mind when he sees Jennie's springy hair. He probably just wonders how it would feel to pull it. But he's smart enough to figure out what I want now.

"What do you think you should do now?"

"Sorry, Jennie," he says, and with this display of genuine remorse and repentance, skips back to his seat. Lesson learned, right?

If I had a do-over, the student meeting about rules would be a little different. I would be less concerned about the beauty of the poster and the seriousness of the signing ceremony, and more concerned about whether the students know exactly what I expect of them. (After all, how many third graders sign legal documents? They write their names on things all the time at school. They don't really know why. They just shrug and do it so they can go to recess.)

I might invite student input on the rules or I might not. In any case, I would make sure to state the expectations in terms of actions (Keep Your Hands to Yourself, instead of Be Kind) and teach each one in many different contexts throughout the year instead of relying on a poster and a special pen to do my work for me.

I have created a program called *Chaos to Confidence* that will lead you step-by-step through the process of creating a routine and teaching it to your students.

Please go to PositiveTeachingStrategies.com and pick up a free copy as my thank you for reading this book!

 **CHAPTER 13**

Love and War

I reminisce about my love for my favorite teacher
and why I kicked her in the shins.

When I was in third grade I was in love with my teacher. She had beautiful long, straight, shiny black hair and green eyes. I had a Miss Blaskowski doll at home. Because I loved her so much, I was a perfect **angel** in her class, right? Yeah, not so much.

I was the kind of kid that never shut up in class. I talked during lessons, I talked during **silent work periods** and during **Sustained Silent Reading**. I not only talked all the time, but I was very active. I ran in the classroom. I knocked over fish tanks and bookshelves. I kicked people. One time I even kicked the PE teacher, another teacher I loved to death. I cut off my bangs with scissors during class. I cut erasers off of pencils and shredded them. I talked back and argued with the teacher. I pulled hair. I was a hellion.

My work area looked like a giant wad of paper wrapped in a desk. Inside I cultivated fake fingernails out of ten little puddles of Elmer's glue. If I didn't get caught, the puddles hardened in a day or two. I pried them up with my scissors, licked the back of each one, and stuck them to my fingers. Lovely!

And remember, my heart was swollen with love for my teacher the whole time.

Now here's me in my first year of teaching. I send each student a "welcome to school" postcard before the school year starts. I go out to recess and play with them. I smile all the time, even when I'm mad. I play games with them, give them gifts and prizes, sing with them, and tell jokes. I praise even their crappiest work and only correct them in the most apologetic way possible. I'm sure many of them love me to death.

Then comes the big letdown. The students misbehave anyway! I know they're just kids and make mistakes, so I pull them aside and tell them how much they hurt my feelings when they act up. Surprisingly this makes absolutely no difference. They apologize and continue doing whatever they want. I'm crushed! Personal rejection!

After awhile their betrayal angers me, and I treat them the way I perceive they treat me. At first, I'm nice one minute and mean the next. Then I hold grudges, getting a student back for a perceived slight days or even weeks later. Later I'm mean pretty much all the time, becoming the nagging, sarcastic teacher I always hated, and the students respond to my malice in kind. It is not a pretty situation.

Was I wrong to try to make learning fun? Play with the students? Sing with them? Give them prizes? Absolutely not! In fact, it's important to treat students with respect, caring, and even love. The problem was I expected the students to pay me back with good **behavior**. And while treating students with respect is a good thing do to, kissing up to them so they will behave is not.

Be friendly with the students but don't try to be friends. You can develop a close relationship with your students but it is a mentor-mentee relationship, not a best friends relationship. Do not punish or reward with affection. Be friendly and caring with your students because they are people, not because of anything they have done or not done.

Kids are still learning how to behave and often don't know why they do what they do. Although some students may be deliberately trying to "push your buttons" or behave "for you," most are not. Kids are **impulsive** and do what feels good to them in the moment. Try not to take it personally.

Behavior is learned just like **long division** is

learned. Students push the **boundaries** so they can learn what is acceptable and what is not. When students make mistakes in their behavior, correct them in the same objective, matter-of-fact way you would correct a long division error. It takes some students awhile to learn long division, and it may take some students awhile to learn correct behavior. Be patient. Above all, keep your cool and try not to be drawn in to the drama of the moment. Remember you are the adult, and students are looking to you to see how a well-put-together adult acts.

 # CHAPTER 14

What's the Matter With Kids These Days?

In which I drink a little, bitch a lot, and learn to lower my expectations.

My teacher friends gather Friday afternoons for a swim at the beach. Afterwards we have dinner and some drinks, trade gossip, and all take turns complaining about the students and their parents.

"Today I caught a girl rolling around on the floor under her desk. When I asked her what she was doing, she just looked at me like she didn't know what I was talking about."

"That's pretty crazy. You know Brian from my class? He actually whistled while I was trying to teach social studies today. Whistled! Then he couldn't believe it when I asked him to stop. When I was in third grade, no way would I whistle in the middle of a lesson. My mom would have grounded me for a week."

"As if it does any good to call the parents. If they answer the phone at all, they act like, what? Can't you do your job? I think kids should come to school at least knowing how to **respect** adults."

"AND how to sit in a chair."

"No kidding! Well all I can say is thank God for rum. You need a refill?"

On and on it would go well into the night. Our students didn't know how to talk to adults, how to read, how to do basic math, how to sit in a chair, put their names on their work, turn in their work, raise their hands, bring a pencil to class, or anything else necessary for their success in school. We blamed the parents, but it was really our fault.

It's unfair to expect students to know how to act without teaching them. How are they supposed to know it's not okay to chase their friend in the classroom or talk to their friends during a video, when it's just fine to do it at recess or at home? Some teachers have no problem with students shouting out answers, and some require hand-raising at all times. What I consider disrespectful, another teacher may think is perfectly fine. If students aren't given specific instructions about what you expect, they will make a guess and push the **boundaries** to the limit to learn what they're supposed to do and what will happen if they don't.

It's best to assume students know nothing when they come to your classroom. If you are wise, one of your first lessons on the first day of school will be "How to Enter the Room," followed shortly by "How to Raise Your Hand" and "How to Address the Teacher." If you are teaching older students, still teach these lessons. Tenth graders need to learn routines at least as urgently as third graders.

Make sure you clearly teach what you don't want, as well as what you do want. Of course it's impossible to anticipate every single way students will push your limits, but try to tighten as many loopholes as possible. With experience you will learn all the common problems and the best ways to stop them before they start. In the meantime, make your best guess and adjust as necessary. When students don't follow your expectations, be sure to firmly correct them right away. If they persist, it's time for a follow-up discussion and/or practice at lunch or after school.

Many resources are available to help you figure out which **behavior lessons** to teach and how to teach them. If you go to PositiveTeachingStrategies.com and join the Positive Educator Community, you will be able to sign up for free video trainings, join webinars and classes, and find out how to hire me to speak at your school. You can also get more great ideas by asking a master teacher at your school or observing a teacher who is really skilled in classroom management. Oh, and the teacher supply store might have some really good books, too!

 **CHAPTER 15**

Guess What? He's Coming Back!

Why didn't the principal fix little Matthew for me?

andreeamironiuc.com

A traffic cop pulls you over and asks for your registration and license. "You were going thirty mph over the speed limit," she informs you.

What do you expect next? A ticket, right? But no!

She says, "If I could, I would write you a ticket. You better watch out! Next time I'm going to send you to the Chief of Police!"

I don't know what you are thinking in this situation, but I know what I'm thinking. "What kind of a cop can't write a speeding ticket? Is she a cop-in-training? Does she write too many tickets, so they took her ticket book away? Maybe she can't write? Lost her pen?"

I'm thinking, "Whew, I'm off the hook! I hope a real cop doesn't pull me over next time." And also "Is this the kind of person protecting my community from the bad guys?"

Now let's take a look at me in my first year of teaching. Matthew, one of my little darlings, throws a paper airplane and it actually hits me in the head. Collective gasp (and a few giggles) from the class. All eyes are on me. Calculating eyes. Watching eyes. Challenging eyes (in the case of Matthew the Plane-Hurler.)

What do I do? I send him to **the office**, of course. Airplane-flinging is clearly defiant **behavior**! He needs to see the principal. That'll solve it!

I'm sure you can see the problem. What is the principal going to do that I couldn't do? Will the principal really suspend little Matthew for throwing a paper airplane? Of course not! In fact, in half an hour Matthew will return to class. Maybe he'll miss a recess. And guess what? He's going to tell all his friends the funny story about how he made the teacher all mad and got out of math by throwing a paper airplane. What fun!

Matthew missed class but he definitely learned a few things at school today. So did the rest of the class. Matthew and the class learned that the teacher turns a really funny color of pink and gets spots on her neck when she gets mad. They learned paper airplanes are not only fun to throw, but are a powerful tool for getting out of class. Above all, they learned the teacher is powerless to "write the ticket." She calls in the principal, who may or may not think it's worth doing anything about. Misbehaving is suddenly a pretty good deal.

Of course, sometimes it's necessary to remove students from class but please, please don't give away your personal power! Try these suggestions instead.

Give students access only to the materials they need for the assignment. Desks should be clear of everything except what they are actually using. If Matthew doesn't have extra paper, it will be harder for him to make a paper airplane. If he does start to fold a piece of paper, look at him and say, "Matthew, please give me the paper." If he doesn't, send him to **time out** and have him fill out a **reflection form** (which he hopefully won't turn into a paper airplane.)

If Matthew is somehow able to create a stealth paper airplane and hits you in the head with it, take a deep breath. Anger and emotionalism add drama, spice, and entertainment. If you lose it, you will lose. After your deep breath, calmly do the time out thing and keep on teaching until you cool down. After time out, assign Matthew a **consequence**, such as picking paper off the floor after class. Do not talk to him about his paper airplane during class. Let him sweat it out and pay the consequences on his own time.

If Matthew refuses to go to time out, fill out his reflection form, or pick up papers after class, call the office and say this: "Matthew needs to take a time out in the office. Please send someone to get him. No, he doesn't need to see the principal. I'll send some work with Matthew, and I'll come get him at recess and talk to him myself." When you do this you will keep your power. You will be the powerful supervisor, directing what is going to happen. All those watching eyes are going to get the message that their teacher is in charge of Matthew, his consequence, and the staff in the office.

As a teacher, you have the power. Don't make the mistake I did. Don't give your power away to anyone, even the principal.

Conclusion and Takeaways

In which I brag about my tan and suggest you wear a helmet.

I arrived in Hawaii with a gazillion boxes of teacher supplies and books, excitement, and optimism. After four years, I acquired lots of great friends, an amazing tan, and about fifteen years of life experience. On the flight back to Honolulu, I knew about half the people on the airplane and understood almost everything they were saying. I still had a gazillion boxes, but now they were filled with kukui nut leis, hand-woven tapa boxes, Ka Hula Piko tee shirts, and the **classroom management** notebooks that saved my life.

I arrived with bravado and came away with confidence. I arrived thinking I could do it all and left grateful for the help of others who were not only more skilled and experienced, but willing to share, coach, and support me. I arrived with a college degree and great grades. I left with enough practical skills to serve me for a lifetime.

Learning to teach and manage a class is like learning to ride a bike. You can be told over and over what to do, but the only way to learn is to do it with the support of training wheels, then an adult running alongside, and then some crashes when you're out on your own. But you don't have to run into a tree or ride against the traffic on the freeway and get creamed by the big semis. Inflate your tires first, and check your brakes. Get a helmet.

I hope my experiences have been eye-opening, entertaining, and helpful to you. I hope you're not as naïve as I was, and I also hope you have some of that optimism and desire to empower and enlighten your students. I hope you are as lucky as me and are able to get help when you need it. And I also hope you are smart enough to reach out and ask for assistance before you hit bottom like I did.

If you have any questions, please feel free to e-mail me at PositiveTeachingStrategies@gmail.com or message me at Facebook.com/PositiveTeachingStrategies. I would be pleased to help as much as I can. When I think of those who picked me up, dusted me off, patched me up, and gave me the tools I needed to succeed, I am grateful. I owe it to them, to you, and to the students we all serve.

'A 'ohe pu 'u ki 'eki 'e ke ho 'â 'o 'ia e pi 'i.
(No cliff is so tall it cannot be scaled.)

Acknowledgments and Apologies

Writing this, I am reminded of a single-actor play I recently enjoyed. Everyone focused on the actor and the story he told, but so many people went into its production. The lighting crew, scriptwriter, director, stage crew, musicians, and sound-effects technicians; the ticket-takers, program designers, printers, producers, and agents; the people who built the theatre and the custodial staff that cares for it. Many, many people went into the seemingly simple experience of one actor telling a story. Although this book is mostly about me, the others in the story are just as important, but not as visible. I can't possibly ac-knowledge everyone, but I'm going to try.

First of all I want to offer a huge apology to all the paper-airplane-hurling students in my class in my first two years. I did a crummy job and I'm sorry. If you can actually read this book, it isn't my fault. Someone else must have helped you out, and I'm glad they did. Of course you didn't exactly make it easy on me, which is why I learned so much. So I guess I need to thank you for the education you gave to me.

For Kelly Field, my buddy at the classroom management class, and a loving and supportive friend in so many ways, thank you.

To Teresa Alsept, roommate and friend, who first introduced me to the "teacher stare," thanks for all your words of wisdom, even though I didn't listen to a lot of them. Turns out you were right most of the time. And you make great red beans and rice, too!

Thanks also to Janet Anderson, teaching partner in my second and third years of teaching. I apologize for disturbing your class with all the noise and chaos in my second year of teaching, and for the patient way you listened to me and encouraged me. Your generous spirit of sharing helped me in ways you will never know.

Thank you Lynette Shafer, priest extraordinaire,

who wouldn't give up on me, no matter what. In case you wondered if being in the ministry makes a difference, I am living proof it does.

To Mom and Dad, who taught me to try my best, never give up, and work hard. Also thank you for not disowning me when I ran off to Hawaii.

A gigantic thank you to Dolores Cook, teacher of the Positive Approaches for Children management class that saved me professionally. I am so grateful for your work and I have fond memories of your powerful class. I apologize for asking so many questions and giving you a headache. Most likely you had to have a big fat Mai-Tai in the hotel bar after teaching the class I attended.

Finally, thank you to my husband, Keith Ayres. You stuck with me even when living with me must have been like living with a dark, life-sucking vacuum cleaner. I'm glad we're together, even though it hasn't been a pretty path at times. Thank you for treating life as a great big adventure and for letting me share it with you. I can't imagine where I'd be without you.

Glossary of Teacher-Speak

Alphabet Chart A long skinny banner with the alphabet printed on it. Usually runs corner to corner near the ceiling in elementary classrooms. Versions vary, depending on grade level and Martha Stewartish tendencies of the teacher. Often populated with animals or objects which start with each letter (such as Ape for A.) Some have been in the same place so long the wall will fall apart if it is taken down.

Angelic Student An angel is a supernatural being of light that provides protection or information. Once I read that angels can also have a pleasing fragrance. Angelic students are quiet, neat, compliant, and usually cute. And come to think of it, they generally smell nice. A certain type of student appears to be an angel at first, but is really just very sneaky and gets away with everything.

Behavior The way students act, especially how well they follow directions and get along with others. Teachers talk about behavior a lot, because it sounds more objective to say "Marcus has behavior issues" than it does to say "Marcus is annoying."

Behavior Lesson In my grandparents' day a behavior lesson was a spanking (as in "I'm going to take you out to the woodshed and teach you a lesson.") Nowadays a behavior lesson is detailed training on what the adult wants the student to do in a specific situation. Great behavior lessons can be fun and can save the teacher hours and hours of time and stress. They also do not require a paddle and rarely produce tears. I highly recommend them.

Behavior Limits see *Boundaries*

Boundaries Lines drawn in the sand which will trigger a consequence if crossed. A boundary can be a literal boundary, such as where students are allowed to sit during Sustained Silent Reading, or a figurative boundary, such as how many times students can sharpen their pencils while the teacher is talking. (I recommend anywhere they want as long as you can see them and zero, respectively.)

Butcher Paper Extra-sturdy paper that comes on gigantic rolls. Used by butchers and fishmongers to wrap meat. Teachers (especially elementary teachers) use a colored version for just about everything, including but not limited to table linens, costumes, posters, window shades, and covering bookshelves at the end of the year so the books don't walk off. The most common teacher use of butcher paper is to cover up the really ugly, pockmarked, baby-poop-brown bulletin boards before decorating them. If you want to see a school-wide teacher panic, kidnap the butcher paper cart two days before school starts.

Class Book A handmade book created collaboratively by the whole class, usually modeled after a "real" book. Often each student will create a page using a template. For instance, the teacher reads *Brown Bear, Brown Bear, What Do You See?* by Bill Martin, Jr., then the class creates *Silver Snake, Silver Snake, What Do You Eat?* (I probably wouldn't actually use that one because it might give some of the students nightmares.)

Classroom Management The art of leading your class. Classroom management includes everything from setting up the classroom so students will succeed to inspiring the students to practice behaviors that will help them in school. It also includes "doing something about it" when students make choices that interfere with their learning or the learning of others, such as throwing a paper airplane at the teacher.

Consequence What happens as the result of a behavior. In education and parenting, "consequence" has become a verb replacing the word "punish," as in "I'll consequence you if you don't stop throwing paper airplanes at me, Matthew."

Cooperating Teachers (see also *Master Teachers*) Teachers who graciously agree to let student teachers work in their classrooms as interns. A good cooperating teacher has the patience of a saint and the tact of a diplomat, and deserves a special breakfast treat every morning and a heartfelt thank-you note after the student-teaching experience is over.

Curriculum The content you teach. Most of the time what you're supposed to cover is laid out in a really hard-to-understand way in a dusty three-ring binder (check the back of your closet for it.) Then there's the textbook or program the district spent thousands of dollars to purchase that the principal says you have to use. It probably doesn't match up with what's in the three-ring binder. This leads to lots of meetings where you argue with the other teachers, the principals, and the district-level gurus about what you are supposed to teach. Try to avoid being appointed to a curriculum committee.

Direct Instruction The teacher explains or shows the students a concept or skill (otherwise known as lecture, or sage on the stage.) Direct instruction is the opposite of discovery or guide on the side, where the students explore or experiment in groups or on their own. Don't think you will be working less during a discovery lesson. You will be working more, as you ask questions to evoke student thinking, manage materials, help "stuck" students, and keep students on task. I was under the mistaken impression that direct instruction was bad and discovery was good, but master teachers have a balance of both.

Discipline Expectations see *Expectations*

Engage Get students involved. Do it as often as possible.

Expectations (otherwise known as *Discipline Expectations*) The mental image the teacher has of the way the students will act in a given situation. Beginning teachers (and many experienced teachers) sometimes make the mistake of assuming the students are already aware of this mental image. Master teachers know that expectations need to be expressed, explained, and demonstrated in detail.

Filler Activities Worksheets, games, and projects that you ask students to do when a lesson takes less time than you think it will. Also used for The Student Who Finishes Everything Early before she starts doing all your prep work for you. The best filler activities enrich or reinforce the skills or concepts the students are currently learning. The worst ones keep the students occupied but are otherwise a waste of time and paper.

Graphic Organizer I know this sounds like a person who swears while cleaning out your closets, but really it's a kind of chart that students use to brainstorm, take notes, or do all sorts of other fun activities. Teachers with Martha Stewartish tendencies spend hours making up really adorable graphic organizers with curlicues and cute letters to go with whatever holiday is coming up. Master teachers show their students how to create their own.

Impulsive Inclined to act on sudden urges, such as pulling another student's hair or kicking the physical education teacher. Impulsiveness happens when a thought is transformed immediately into action without getting flight clearance from Mission Control. This, unfortunately for teachers, is how all kids (and a lot of adults) learn behavior limits.

Integrated Unit A series of lessons and/or a project which requires several different content area skills to complete. When I was in seventh grade, we did a fantastic integrated unit where we designed a car trip. We used reading, research skills, map-reading, science, art, and math. It was great! In my first year of teaching, I designed lame math worksheets filled with story problems about bugs for my infamous insect unit. It was not great. (See also *Unit* and *Thematic Unit*.)

Long Division A way to divide large numbers that students used to learn a million years ago before the invention of the calculator. Now students resist learning long division because the calculator is easier and faster—assuming they put the right numbers in (which they usually don't.)

Master Teachers Teachers who have been teaching a long time and know their stuff. Cooperating Teachers are also often referred to as master teachers.

Motivation The inspiration for an action. There is

a lot of talk in education circles about whether it's okay for students to be motivated by rewards and consequences or whether they should be self-motivated. To me this is like talking about whether the moon should show up in the sky during the day. Even if it seems like it shouldn't, it does, and there's not much you can do about it.

The Office The portion of the school which houses the principal and the principal's staff. Also used casually to mean the people who work in the office, as in "I'm going to call the office." One thing to remember about the office is that the principal, discipline coordinator, and/or counselor are often in meetings or away from the school. If you send students to the office, they may be supervised by receptionists, secretaries, nurses, or parent volunteers who are already busy with their own work and have little or no training for working with students. If you expect the office to "fix" your students, you will be disappointed.

Plan Time (also known as *Prep Time*) Time during

a work day when you're not in charge of students and are supposedly able to concentrate on figuring out what and how to teach them. Often taken up with senseless meetings, parent conferences or e-mail, or providing extra help to students who need it.

Planning Setting up schedules, figuring out the best way to teach your curriculum, and establishing systems and procedures for your room to run efficiently. Planning does NOT include making copies, putting up bulletin boards, arranging furniture, or making an outfit for the teddy bear in the reading area. These activities are officially prep work and can often be skipped or outsourced.

Pokémon An evil invention of Satan for the torture of teachers. Students who are into Pokémon think of nothing else. They buy, trade, and steal cards from each other to get the best possible combination of characters and powers so they can attack each other in a war game at recess and gamble on the outcome. Pokémon cards cause so many problems at school they are almost universally banned. If they aren't banned from your school, do yourself a favor and ban them from your class anyway.

Reflection Form A form that students fill out when they are removed from class for disruptive behavior. When done correctly, a reflection form can be a helpful learning experience for students. When used as a punishment, it is ineffective and leads to even more disruptive behavior.

Respect When students defer to adults because of trust (or in some cases, fear.) Some teachers believe students should automatically respect them and are resentful if they don't.

Silent Work Period Do you believe in silent work periods? How about Santa Claus? (My answer is YES! I believe in both!)

Staff Room A break room for teachers and other staff at a school. A million years ago, the teachers used to go there to smoke. My science teacher in high school used to come out of the staff room trailing a blue cloud. Thank goodness it's different now. Now the only toxic thing you have to watch out for in the staff room is the Negative Teacher Who Complains About Everything. Like The Student Who Finishes Everything Early, you will identify her on the first day of school.

Student Teacher A college student studying to be a teacher and interning under the direct supervision of an established teacher. Student teachers are observed and graded by their college professors and are also evaluated by their supervising teacher. Student teaching used to be called practice teaching, which in some ways is a pretty good description. The main ways you can spot student teachers are by their boundless enthusiasm and their gigantic notebooks filled with college paperwork. Also their coffee-stain-free teeth.

Subject Area Content see *Curriculum*

Sustained Silent Reading (SSR) Also known as DEAR (Drop Everything And Read,) ZYLAR (Zip Your Lips And Read,) FUR (Free Uninterrupted Reading,) and about a million other acronyms,

Sustained Silent Reading is a time each day when students read whatever they want, just for fun. Teachers are also supposed to be able to read during this time, which would be nice if it ever happened. They usually don't get to because it might be the only time they can check their e-mail to see if any parents have written to express a "concern" (which is code for something they want to yell at you for.) Another problem is if the books the teachers really want to read are inappropriate for the students to see them reading, or if teachers must use the time to do the lesson plan they didn't have time to do during their prep time because the principal called an emergency meeting to discuss the bus schedule AGAIN.

Thematic Unit A series of lessons based on a theme such as The Rainforest or Insects. They can last anywhere from a day to a month. Thematic units that go well can be remembered fondly by the students for years. Thematic units that go poorly make teachers and students so sick of the theme that they hope they never have to read, see, or hear anything about the topic ever again. These units will unfortunately also be remembered by students and teachers for years. (See also *Unit* and *Integrated Unit.*)

Time Out Removing students from the class for a short time to calm down and reflect on their behavior. It can also be a place, as in "I'm putting you in Time Out." I read one book where it was likened to the penalty box in ice hockey, only not as cold.

Unit Even though it sounds like something out of a sci-fi movie, a unit is actually a series of lessons about a specific topic or theme. (See also *Thematic Unit* and *Integrated Unit.*)

Work Sample Project A college requirement for student teachers containing detailed plans for a unit they will deliver to the class they are practicing on. It usually has a lot of silly requirements (such as an index) which have little or nothing to do with actually planning a school year or creating lesson plans. My own work sample project was a fifty-two page weeklong unit about insects. I had to buy an extra-large D-ring notebook for it. I mistakenly thought my insect unit would be useful in my first year of teaching. I was wrong.

About the Author

Katrina Ayres has been teaching more than sixteen years. She has a passion for enriching the classroom experiences of educators and students.
Katrina has created videos, webinars, and books for teachers and student teachers. As a Certified Time to Teach Associate Trainer with the Center for Teacher Effectiveness, Katrina speaks at conventions and workshops all over the United States. Please contact her if you are interested in hiring her to train at your school or speak at your workshop.

Web: *PositiveTeachingStrategies.com*
Email: *PositiveTeachingStrategies@gmail.com*
Facebook: *Facebook.com/PositiveTeachingStrategies*

About the Illustrator

Andreea Mironiuc is a Romanian illustrator located in Odense, Denmark. She loves travel, chocolate, and freelance projects. To contact Andreea or view her portfolio, visit her website at http://www.andreeamironiuc.com.

Resources

Nothing will help you learn classroom management skills better than working closely with an experienced mentor or coach, or taking a class from a classroom management expert who is also a classroom teacher. However, books and do-it-yourself programs can help if in-person training is not available to you. Contact me at PositiveTeachingStrategies@gmail.com *if you would like me to speak at your event or train at your school.*

Time To Teach: Encouragement, Empowerment, and Excellence in Every Classroom by Rick Dahlgren, Judy Hyatt, and Carolyn Dobbins (1997).

Effective teachers realize that good discipline begins with the "little stuff." This book describes how prompt attention to the "little stuff" can prevent the "big stuff" — that is, how good timing is the key to effective discipline. The research-based strategies in this book are easy to implement and ready to use.

Retails for $24.99. Contact me directly at *Positive TeachingStrategies@gmail.com* for a twenty percent discount.

Teach-To's: 100 Behavior Lesson Plans and Essential Advice by Rick Dahlgren (2007).

In addition to the one hundred Teach-To's™ in this book, a powerful format is provided to help you develop your own behavioral lesson plans so your students can learn all the skills they will need to be successful in your classroom. Learn what to do in the first month, first week, and first day of school, times critical to classroom management.

Retails for $49.95. Contact me directly at *Positive TeachingStrategies@gmail.com* for a twenty percent discount.

Learn from my own teacher, **Dolores Cook of Positive Approaches for Children**, 800-933-8582, who provides individual coaching for teachers.

Chaos to Confidence: 5 Steps to Gain Control of Your Class and Enjoy Teaching Again audio mini-workshop by Katrina Ayres.

This audio program will teach you how to create a classroom routine that is complete and ready for you to implement; how to determine which chaos-causing activity to tackle first, so you can reduce your stress and increase your confidence right away; how to systematically teach classroom routines to your students so that they will challenge you less and your relationship with them will improve; and how to reinforce your routine so your classroom will continue to hum with productivity and organization all the way through to the end of the school year.

FREE with when you join my Positive Educator Community. Pick yours up now at *PositiveTeaching Strategies.com.*

Made in the USA
Charleston, SC
16 February 2015